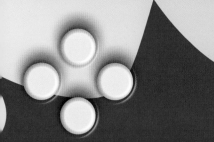

League of Legends

Beginner's Guide

21st Century Skills **INNOVATION LIBRARY**

Josh Gregory

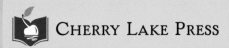

Published in the United States of America by Cherry Lake Publishing Group
Ann Arbor, Michigan
www.cherrylakepublishing.com

Reading Adviser: Beth Walker Gambro, MS, Ed., Reading Consultant, Yorkville, IL

Cherry Lake Press is an imprint of Cherry Lake Publishing Group.

Library of Congress Cataloging-in-Publication Data

Names: Gregory, Josh, author.
Title: League of legends : beginner's guide / by Josh Gregory.
Description: Ann Arbor, Michigan : Cherry Lake Publishing, [2023] | Series: Unofficial guides. 21st century
    skills innovation library | Includes bibliographical references and index. | Audience: Grades 4-6 | Summary:
    "Though it was originally developed by a small independent team, League of Legends has grown to become
    the biggest game in all of esports, with high-stakes matches that draw as many viewers as pro football games.
    This book will help readers get started in their own League of Legends careers with helpful hints, strategies,
    and much more. Includes table of contents, author biography, sidebars, glossary, index, and informative
    backmatter"— Provided by publisher.
Identifiers: LCCN 2023002168 (print) | LCCN 2023002169 (ebook) | ISBN 9781668927939 (library binding) |
    ISBN 9781668928981 (paperback) | ISBN 9781668930458 (epub) | ISBN 9781668933411 (kindle edition) |
    ISBN 9781668931936 (pdf)
Subjects: LCSH: League of legends (Video game)—Juvenile literature.
Classification: LCC GV1469.37 .G745 2023 (print) | LCC GV1469.37 (ebook) | DDC 794.8—dc23/eng/20230124
LC record available at https://lccn.loc.gov/2023002168
LC ebook record available at https://lccn.loc.gov/2023002169

Cherry Lake Publishing Group would like to acknowledge the work of the Partnership for 21st Century Learning,
a Network of Battelle for Kids. Please visit http://www.battelleforkids.org/networks/p21 for more information.

Printed in the United States of America

Note from publisher: Websites change regularly, and their future contents are outside of our control. Supervise children when conducting any recommended online searches for extended learning opportunities.

Josh Gregory is the author of more than 200 books for kids. He has written about everything from animals to technology to history. A graduate of the University of Missouri–Columbia, he currently lives in Chicago, Illinois.

Contents

CHAPTER 1

A Legendary Game

What kinds of video games do you like? Are you into fast-paced competitive multiplayer action? What about careful strategy? Maybe you're most interested in roleplaying games where you get to build up a customized character and make them stronger. But wait. What if there was a game with all of those styles mixed together?

If that sounds like a fun time, *League of Legends* might be the right game for you. *League of Legends* is a type of game called a multiplayer online battle arena, or MOBA for short. The first MOBA was created back in 2003. Amazingly, it wasn't built by a team of professional **developers**. Instead, it was a fan-created **mod** for the strategy game *Warcraft III*. Titled *Defense of the Ancients* and better known as *Dota* to fans, the mod pitted two teams against each other. The teams started out in opposite corners of a square map. The goal was simply to reach the other team's corner and destroy a structure called an Ancient. Over the course of a match, each player could defeat enemies to level up and grow stronger.

Though it seemed simple on the surface, this combination of action, strategy, and roleplaying proved to have a lot of depth. *Dota* became a runaway success, with players constantly finding new strategies and techniques.

Other MOBAs, such as *Dota 2*, will look very familiar after playing *League of Legends*.

Riot Games Strikes Again

As Riot Games has grown along with its signature game, its developers have also worked to launch other games. Its biggest success so far outside of *League of Legends* has been a first-person shooter called *Valorant*. Released in 2020, it's a team-based competitive online game in which players can choose from a number of unique playable characters called heroes, much like the champions in *League of Legends*. Almost immediately, the game became a huge hit. It regularly ranks among the most-viewed games on streaming services and has been a breakout success on the esports scene, proving that Riot Games was more than just a one-hit wonder.

It became a fixture of professional **esports** tournaments. Soon, professional game developers began trying to create their own takes on this surprisingly popular fan-made game. Blizzard Entertainment, the creators of *Warcraft III* and several other incredibly popular games, created a game called *Heroes of the Storm*. Valve Software, the PC gaming powerhouse behind *Counter-Strike* and *Team Fortress*, hired the creators of *Dota* and created *Dota 2*. But even with these major game developers creating MOBAs, it was once again a small, independent team that had the biggest success.

In 2006, Brandon "Ryze" Beck and Marc "Tryndamere" Merrill decided to start a game development company called Riot Games. The two had met as college roommates and shared a passion for *Dota*. They wanted to create their own MOBA—one that players would stick with for years to come, rather than moving on to the latest thing every time a new game came out.

Valorant is a very different kind of game than *League of Legends*, but it keeps the fast-paced esports action Riot Games is famous for.

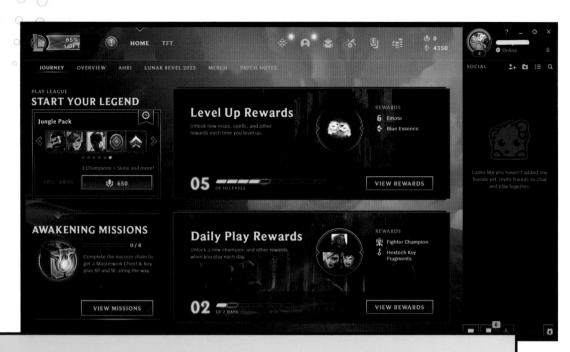

The main menu of *League of Legends* might look intimidating at first, but you will soon learn how everything works.

After several years of hard work and several months of **beta tests**, Riot Games released *League of Legends* as a free download in October 2009. Through word of mouth among gamers online, the game gradually grew in popularity. More than a decade later, it has grown to become one of the biggest games in the world. Beck and Merrill got exactly what they had hoped for: a game that players would play for years and years. At any given point, millions of people are logged in and playing, with countless others watching streams through Twitch or similar services. It is far and away the most popular MOBA today.

Though Riot Games started off small, the success of *League of Legends* has helped it grow. Today, it has thousands of employees and offices all around the world, much like the massive companies it competed with in the beginning. It's one of the biggest gaming success stories in recent history.

So what's all the fuss about? Why not try the game for yourself and find out? You'll face stiff competition online from the players who have been at it for years, but you're also bound to have a lot of fun while you're at it.

League of Legends is always action-packed.

CHAPTER 2

Stay in Your Lane

It's easy to get started with *League of Legends*. All you need are a Windows or Mac PC and a fast internet connection. The game is a free download. Once you've installed it, all you need to do is create an account and log in.

The first time you start *League of Legends*, you will be dropped into a short tutorial. It's a good idea to pay close attention here. *League of Legends* is a complex game, and it can be very difficult to master. Even learning the basics will take some time, but the built-in tutorial does a good job of showing you how to play before you jump online to face off against real-life players.

The main mode in *League of Legends* is called Summoner's Rift. Each match takes place on the same map, so you'll learn its layout quickly. There will be two teams, each with five players. One team starts in the bottom-left corner, while another starts in the top-right corner. The basic goal is simple: reach the opposing team's corner and destroy a structure called the Nexus, all while protecting your own Nexus. But of course, the game is not nearly as simple as it seems.

Your Nexus looks like this. Keeping it safe is the most important thing if enemies get close to your starting area.

When the circle around a turret turns red, the turret is getting ready to attack you. Get out as soon as you can!

Each team's Nexus is protected by towers called turrets. These towers are located in specific locations on the map. They will attack any enemies who get too close. In addition, each team's Nexus will spawn a series of computer-controlled creatures called minions. Minions will move toward the opposing team's Nexus, attacking enemy players, minions, and turrets in their path.

The map has three lanes connecting the two teams' Nexuses: one at the top, one at the bottom, and one straight across the center of the map. Turrets are located along these lanes, and minions will travel along the lanes as well. The areas in between the lanes are known as the jungle. In the jungle, you will find neutral monsters who will attack either team's players if they get too close.

The main flow of a match is that players will proceed down a lane and try to defeat each turret that stands in the way. Behind the first couple of turrets, you will find a device called an inhibitor. Destroying the inhibitor

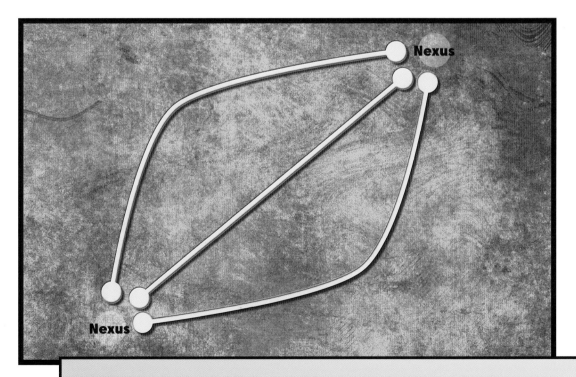

Nexus

Nexus

Learning the basic structure of the Summoner's Rift map is a very important part of playing *League of Legends*.

does a couple of important things. First, it allows your team's Nexus to begin spawning more powerful minions, called super minions. Second, it causes two special turrets called Nexus turrets to pop up near the opposing team's Nexus. These two turrets need to be defeated before your team can do damage to the enemy Nexus.

As you move across the map, you'll notice that you can only see a certain distance around your character. The rest of the screen will be covered in a dark shadow. This is called the fog of war. It also affects the minimap

Once you destroy an inhibitor, you will get a message letting you know that super minions are on the way to help you.

Staying Safe

Like most team-based games, *League of Legends* offers players a number of ways to communicate as they play. If you are playing with friends you know from real life, it can be nice to use the game's voice chat to talk during matches. But if you are playing with strangers, it's best to go to the options menu and turn this feature off. This way you won't have to worry about accidentally revealing personal information to a stranger. You also won't need to listen to annoying people yelling into their microphones. Best of all, you can still communicate with your teammates by using the game's "ping" system to mark locations, enemies, and other important points of interest so your teammates can investigate.

in the corner of your screen. You can see the area around your character, friendly minions, and teammates. But you won't know what's happening in the fogged areas unless you physically move into them. This keeps teams from spying on each other from a distance.

Most teams will send one player along the top lane, one through the center, and two along the bottom. It's important to cover all three to keep opposing teams from getting through. You'll need a balance of defense and offense to win.

CHAPTER 3

Choose Your Champion

One of the things that keeps players coming back to *League of Legends* year after year is that there are dozens of different characters to play as. Each character, or champion, has different strengths and weaknesses and a completely unique set of moves to learn. This means if you get bored of one, you can start trying to learn the ins and outs of another. When the game first launched in 2009, there were 40 champions to choose from. Today, there are more than 140, with more being added all the time.

It's not a good idea to constantly switch from one champion to another when you are first learning to play *League of Legends*. Instead, it's best to pick a "main" and stick with them, learning all the details of their abilities. Even highly experienced players often have a main, even if they are able to play well as a few others characters too. In other words, it pays to **specialize**.

Which champion should you pick? When you're a beginner, you may as well just choose whichever one looks most interesting to you. The game assigns a difficulty rating to each champion, based on how complicated they are to use. But no matter what, there's going to be a learning curve. This means you will probably lose a few times before you start winning matches.

At the start of a match, you can see which champions your teammates are choosing. This will help you plan a strategy.

Each champion has a basic attack called an auto attack. You can use this by simply right-clicking on an enemy. Some characters have very fast auto attacks, while others are slow. Some are powerful, while others are less so. You can use auto attacks as much as you want, with no limits.

Champions also come with five unique abilities. One is a passive ability. This means it is always active. It provides some sort of special bonus. For example, one champion

Auto attacks are great for fighting basic minions.

Some abilities take time to activate, and a timer bar
will appear to show you how long you have to wait.

might get a burst of speed after defeating an enemy.
Another might gain extra defense in certain situations.

The champion's other four abilities can be activated
by pressing keys on your keyboard. Many of them are
special attacks. Some can also heal or provide bonuses
to you or your teammates. Each has a cooldown timer.
This means you have to wait a certain amount of time
after using an ability to use it again.

In addition to your champion's built-in abilities, you'll also be able to choose two spells to use in each match. All of the champions can use the same spells. Like abilities, some spells are magic attacks, while others can heal or provide other bonuses.

Combat in *League of Legends* involves a blend of careful strategy and fast action. You'll need to move around, make decisions, and target enemies without wasting any time. But you'll also need to think hard about the timing of your abilities. For example, imagine you have a healing spell. Your character takes a little bit of damage, so you use the spell. But now you have to wait for the cooldown timer to use it again. In the meantime, you take a much larger amount of damage, but now you can't heal. Or imagine you use your most powerful attack to destroy a weak minion. Then, before the cooldown timer ends, a powerful enemy appears out of nowhere, leaving you with fewer options to attack. The trick is to use abilities at the correct time, but don't neglect to use them entirely.

As you defeat enemies during a match, you will earn experience points, or XP. Once you earn enough XP, you will go up a level. Each time this happens, you can choose to improve one of your abilities. This is an important part of winning matches. Your opponents will be growing stronger throughout the match, so you'll need to keep up. Fight minions early on to gain quick XP.

Hover your mouse over an ability to learn more, including its cooldown time, which is shown at the top-right of the info box.

Another way to get quick XP is to head into the jungle areas to fight monsters. One thing to remember is that you'll start each match back at level one—*League of Legends* is not like traditional roleplaying games where you are constantly improving a single character over hours and hours of playtime.

Dressed for Success

Like other popular online games, *League of Legends* offers players a wide variety of unlockable cosmetic items that can be used to customize their champions. There are hundreds of different skins in the game, with new ones being added all the time. Some of them can be purchased through the in-game store using Riot Points. Riot Points cost real-life money to purchase, so always ask an adult before buying anything in the game. You can also earn cosmetics simply by playing the game. Playing matches and completing missions will earn you something called Blue Essence. This valuable material can be traded for all kinds of in-game items.

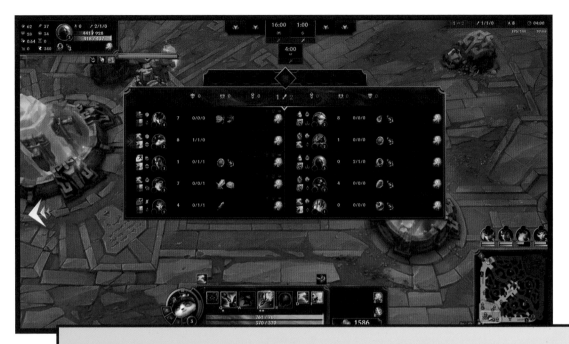

At any point, you can check to see what levels your teammates and opponents are.

Abilities aren't the only things that affect your character's power. Each champion also has a different set of **stats**. These numbers indicate a champion's strengths and weaknesses. For example, a character with a high armor stat is good at absorbing damage from physical attacks like sword swings. (That means their health won't fall so quickly.) But a character with high magic resistance will be better at absorbing attacks from magic spells.

In addition to XP, defeating enemies also earns you gold. If you are in the starting area near your teams Nexus, you can access a shop where you can spend this gold on items that make your character stronger by increasing different stats. For players who are still learning the game, the shop will recommend items for you to buy. This comes in handy when you are trying to

Hover your mouse over each character stat to learn more about what it does.

The recommended items in the shop are almost always a good choice until you are experienced enough to have detailed, advanced strategies that require certain gear.

make decisions in the middle of a hectic match. Just like leveling up abilities, these purchases (and the amount of gold you have) will be reset back to zero at the end of each match.

Don't worry if all of this sounds like a lot to learn. It is! But with a little practice it will be as simple as riding a bicycle.

CHAPTER 4

Spectator Sports

Believe it or not many serious *League of Legends* fans don't really spend much time playing the game themselves. Instead, they join in the fun by watching the pros in action and following along with other events related to the game.

Esports has grown rapidly in popularity in recent years, and *League of Legends* is the most popular esport of all. It is routinely one of the most-watched games on Twitch, and special events can draw truly massive audiences. For example, in 2019, one tournament championship had around 100 million viewers—a similar number to the Super Bowl, and far more than the championships for other traditional sports.

Perhaps the biggest *League of Legends* competition is the *League of Legends* World Championship, a yearly competition sponsored by Riot Games. Riot Games operates twelve official pro esports leagues around the world, and the top teams from each league face off in the World Championship each year. There are millions of dollars of prizes on the line each time. Some of the best players on these pro teams earn more than a million dollars a year playing the game.

You can sometimes watch live esports matches right from the main menu of *League of Legends*.

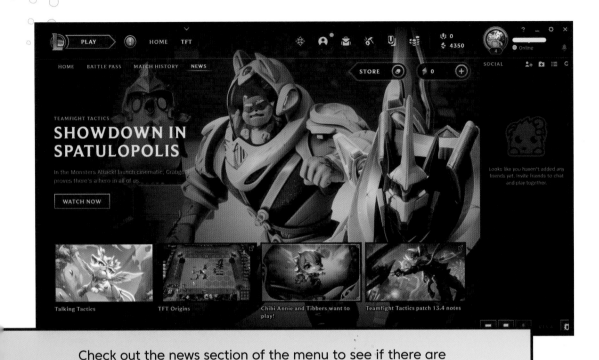

Check out the news section of the menu to see if there are new story-related videos or other media to check out.

For fans whose favorite parts of the game are the characters and setting, Riot Games has also launched a number of multimedia projects set in the *League of Legends* world. Fans keep up with the action reading Marvel's *League of Legends* comic book series and watching *Arcane*, a Netflix animated series set in the *League of Legends* world. There is even an official *League of Legends* heavy metal band called Pentakill that has released several albums. The band is officially made up of several *League of Legends* champion characters, but the actual music is played by a number of famous musicians.

League of Legends fans love collecting toys, clothing, and other gear based on the game.

Keep practicing and victory will soon be yours!

No matter what part of the game you like most, there is always something new to enjoy about *League of Legends*. And with the game's audience always growing, it's never a bad time to jump in and try it for yourself. You never know—you could be the next star player on the esports scene!

A Different Way to Play

In addition to *League of Legends*, Riot Games has created several other games set in the same universe. Each one uses characters and settings from *League of Legends* put into a different video game genre. For example, *Ruined King* is a traditional roleplaying game, while *Legends of Runeterra* is a virtual collectible card game. There is even a mobile phone version of *League of Legends* itself, called *League of Legends: Wild Rift*. Riot Games has promised to keep developing more games in the *League of Legends* world, so fans will have plenty to look forward to.

GLOSSARY

beta tests (BAY-tuh TESTS) final tests before releasing a video game, sometimes conducted by inviting fans to try a game before it is officially released

developers (dih-VEL-uh-purz) people who make video games or other computer programs

esports (EE-sports) organized, professional video game competitions

mod (MAHD) fan-made additions to games

skins (SKINS) different appearances your character can take on in a video game

specialize (SPEH-shuh-lyze) to focus on doing one thing very well instead of doing several things at an average level

stats (STATS) numerical measurements of different strengths and weaknesses

FIND OUT MORE

Books

Gregory, Josh. *Careers in Esports*. Ann Arbor, MI: Cherry Lake Publishing, 2021.

Loh-Hagan, Virginia. *Video Games. In the Know: Influencers and Trends*. Ann Arbor, MI: 45th Parallel Press, 2021.

Orr, Tamra. *Video Sharing. Global Citizens: Social Media*. Ann Arbor, MI: Cherry Lake Press, 2019.

Reeves, Diane Lindsey. *Do You Like Getting Creative? Career Clues for Kids*. Ann Arbor, MI: Cherry Lake Press, 2023.

Websites

With an adult, learn more online with these suggested searches.

League of Legends
Check out the official *League of Legends* site to download the game and check out the latest updates.

LoL Esports
Keep up with the latest *League of Legends* esports matches at the official site.

INDEX